Demons Exposed

by

Tim Thompson

© Copyright 2011, Tim Thompson

All Rights Reserved.

No part of this book may be reproduced, stored in a retrieval system, or transmitted by any means, electronic, mechanical, photocopying, recording, or otherwise, without written permission from the author.

ISBN: 978-1-936750-59-7

This book I really want to humbly thank those that have been really standing with me, through the battles, the tears and the pain. I am so blessed to have the friends that I have, because my friends are real. See so many people in life you have to impress them either with your intelligence, money, power, or material items but not my dear friends. So instead of giving a long list of people who could dedicate this book to I want to dedicate this book to those that I have touched my heart and yet know about my past and they know what it's like to be around me and they except me right where I am. But what amazes me is if I have a question about something in life not one of them have ever looked down on me because I didn't know.

First off to my loving lord and savoir. Lord Jesus Christ, I can't begin to say thank you enough or just how grateful I am you came through my ceiling and touched my life. I am so grateful that you have called me by name to know you.

To my loving wife, I know being married to me hasn't been easy in any way at all. Having a husband that sees demons on a regular basis I know must be weird and having a husband that doesn't know at times how to say the right things at the right time isn't easy either. But I will say this, even though we have had to go through countless battles and we have had to fight to get back what the enemy has stolen, there isn't one person I would ever want to do it with but you. You are my best friend, my soul mate, you are my rock at times and you are my helper at understanding people. I find you an incredible woman of God that just keeps growing and becoming more and more an exciting woman of God. Thank you for being there for me and letting me just lean on you in so many ways.

Jeremy, ever sense I met you at E.T. I have felt accepted. I honor and deeply respect you because you have been closer than a brother to me.

Mellic, I have such a great amount of respect for the woman of God you are. I am amazed that I can call you and just say I need help spelling this word or that word and yet you have not ever treated me less. When I needed help finding something in the word you have always been there for me. At times you had to call me back but you did. I feel so honored knowing you because I see the woman of God you are.

Braden, during the course of men of destiny I know I must have called you almost every night and almost every day just wanting to just say this is to intense but yet no matter how many times I called you, you never looked down on me for my past and you never judged me for the things I just needed to let out. I have so much respect for you because you keep it very simple and yet very real all at the same time. I can't thank you enough for just being there so I could try to figure it all out and make it through that class. I admire and respect the man of God you are. Thanks so much ….

Pastor Wilkie, thank you so much for excepting me and letting me be apart of your flock. I know so many pastors don't want some one with my type of past in their church but you have accepted me sense day one. I honor and admire you for the true man of God you are.

Doug, I know when I asked you to help me get this book be edited correctly you were very hesitant about it at first but I knew in my heart that things were going to turn out great with you helping me. Thank you so much for so many long hours editing, correcting, and proof reading and on top of every thing else making sure that this book is inspiring. So for all the hard work you have done thank you.

Joshua, Thank you fore so many things, you are keeping the web sight looking great, your keeping up with my post and updates on the web sight. Thank you for editing this book, reading over it, helping me with words and helping me make sense of my sentences at times, thank you for sowing in to this ministry and thanks for wanting to help in every way, But above all things, thanks for being my friend. I can turn to you and know that you are there for me and the ministry. Thank you so much……

Doug...H, Hey I just want you to know that even when you're busy at work, I understand but the e mails have meant a great amount to me still because its so nice knowing some one relates so well with me. Thank you for sowing in to this minestry, but above all thanks for being my friend.

Dr. Dean Helland, I find you such an incredible man of God. Your friendship means the world to me.......

Pastor Rod, you don't know much about me but when I needed a friend you were there to listen, when I needed genuine advice you were there, when I wanted to just voice my opinion you were there. So pastor thank you so much for letting me reach out to you when so many others didn't see I just needed a friend. I appreciate and respect you a great deal ......

Dennis thanks for helping this ministry.

Thank you so much Lily,your team and all those at Yorkshire for all the hard work you all have given me with all 3 of my books.

DEMONS EXPOSED

I realize what you are about to read might seem intense or it might seem scary, but in reality it's not if you will humble yourself and come to know the power, love and authority you have in Christ Jesus. Please realize this book is based on truth. In several of the letters, I realize it's hard to comprehend at times just how evil and cruel Satan and all his Demons are, but it is a fact of life. John 10:10 states the enemy came to steal, kill and destroy.

    I have personally seen dozens of marriages destroyed, lives destroyed, careers destroyed, companies destroyed, and many dreams and hopes shattered in a matter of seconds. No matter what a T.V. evangelist says, or a pastor says, or what your friends say, Satan and all his demons and all his earthly followers are 100% real. They really do exist. Some people will try to convince you Satan isn't real, but if it's in the word of God its true.

    This book wasn't written to scare you or bring any harm to you, but to wake you up to the fact that there is a real intense war going on over our very souls, and every day it's getting worse. I have met dozens of Christians who have fallen away from the living gospel of Jesus Christ to join occults. Many have decided that Mormonism, Jehovah Witnesses, or some other strange religion is better. Or they throw their walk with Jesus Christ away because some beautiful young woman came into their life and they decided to start serving sex, or another human, thinking that was better than serving and loving Jesus Christ.

There are thousands of reasons and excuses not to serve Jesus Christ, but Hell is a real place for those that decide to serve themselves or Satan. I have had 5 visions of Hell and it is beyond any cruelty or anything any one can imagine, but through God's grace I am not there. I wrote this book to point out that life does have a lot of wonderful pleasures. I have had to battle my flesh in many ways because I was a person who got caught up into extreme sinful behaviors. But when I cried out to Christ, he rescued me from sever torment because, not only was I going insane; I served many spirits that were against God.

This book is not to be taken lightly, but I do pray it will put the fear of God in people because time is running out and we as humans need to watch and pray because the Anti-Christ is coming. Are you ready? Many pastors and others would ask why a Christian would write a book that deals with so much evil and despair. So many Christians have handed over their mind and body to demonic powers because the flesh really enjoys sin. Many Christians have forgotten to stand in the power of God because they have fallen asleep, or become complacent. Too many lives are being destroyed and too many people are just sitting back asking: why, dear God, why did you allow this to happen? Life is very painful at times, but when we hurt inside, we forget that Christ Jesus shed his blood on a cross for us. He became sin for us, so we can have victory over the attacks of the enemy, but we must remain faithful, accountable and teachable at all times.

So many people are taking their own lives now, so many divorces, killings, children being abused, child killings and domestic violence. All these problems are so far out of control: prisons filling up within weeks after being built, juvenile detention centers over flowing, and insane asylums having to be built on a regular basis. Plus, pastors are being shot now, churches being burned down, while so many Christians sit back and wonder why. The hour is past due that we pray for our brothers and sisters in Christ. We need to speak blessings over our pastors and pray for them daily. Church, the time is now to drop to our knees and pray, and just keep praying. Pray in your car, in the shower, at lunch, or wherever you can, but Church, we need to desperately seek and cry out to God.

When a person dies, there are no second chances, there is no redemption, and there is no pleading for mercy from God for them. When you die, if you do not have a personal relationship with Jesus Christ, the true and living God, you are going to go to hell. So, even though this book might offend some one, I want to bring the reality of just how cruel Satan is and just how many humans Satan wants to go to hell with him. Because Satan knows that when a person goes to hell it's over; there's nothing that person can do or say that will make a difference. So, please repent of your sins and ask Jesus Christ into your heart because time is running out.

CHAPTER 1

THE BIG TAKE OVER

Dear Lust,

Pastor Mark will be moving soon to Butte, Montana. He and his wife are so excited that they are taking over a church there because the former pastor retired. So, you are to stand your ground there at all cost, you have done great things in the past. I have heard you have put it into people's minds that having sex with an animal is a great sexual experience, and it will bring much pleasure to them.

This pastor is a threat in many ways, but one area that he keeps very well hidden is he likes short, skinny little blonds that are in their 20s or 30s; even his accountability team knows nothing about this. So, work on this a lot and really convince him that it's OK to keep little dark secrets to himself, so no one will think less of him. Remember, the more he keeps in the dark the more we have access to him. Let's just hope he doesn't ever realize this. He just got a letter about his high school reunion so, I hope you have someone already lined up there as he goes and sees that someone special that you can deceive so, his heart will think a lot about her.

I got word that Raw did a wonderful job with Anger, Strife, Depression and Loneliness in Seattle, WA. They convinced a 16 year old boy how worthless he was and how it was God that took his mom while she was driving drunk. The young man did much more than we ever planned, he raped and beat his girlfriend then went to his school and killed his history teacher; it was such a beautiful thing. I guess they tried their hardest to convince the young man to kill himself, but he didn't. They messed up that great opportunity, but at least now his life is worthless to many, so we can just ignore him for a while. I know Satan, our father, will send in Suicide to take him out because Depression was told to work on him day and night.

Now don't forget that pastor Michael is a threat. So much of our success in Butte, Montana is because of our dear friend Oppression. He has done such a great job there, that we even have Christians taking their life now and claiming there is no hope. What a great thing to be able to deceive so many into thinking that their God can't help them.

I got a letter from Beelzebub. He has let me know a major secret; many people in Hollywood and TV. Producers are being allowed to see things in the spirit. Things that we want them to see, because all these people throughout the United States that we are holding in bondage need to get more information about wizards, mediums, fairies, psychics, and witchcraft. We are waging a full scale attack, using all the deception we can.

You might have heard also that more porn is being made and sold today; more than ever before throughout the world. I heard you were promoted to general now, congrats this is very exciting. Because you really helped destroy thousands of ministries, marriages and lives.

Because of porn, many men say they can't control themselves, because porn has such a hold on them. I am just so thankful they're blinded to why Christ died on the cross and where they can access so much power in that Holy Bible because; if they ever find this out we are done.

Remember, there is a strong resistance against us in Texas, so we need to continuously stand as strong as we can. I just got word Alabama is making a strong effort to come against many of us, and so is Oklahoma. Time is running out and we need to take as many souls with us as possible to hell. As I continue to implant into minds that sodomy is great and sadomasochism isn't wrong, the more ruthless and crude I can convince people to be.

You must continue to realize that I have to have a door way to access the minds of these people so I can continue to further the god of this world and his kingdom. Plus, more accidental deaths are occurring through these minds that I have depraved, which is just so funny knowing that a person was looking for an awesome sexual experience, ended up dying because of it. Plus, I am implanting into people's minds that have money that they need to open an adult toy store. I am just so thrilled how many have died through erotic asphyxiation. It's incredible; these humans are much more stupid than I thought. I just drop an idea in their head and they do it. So many humans just do just what I drop into their mind, no matter how cruel or wicked it seems. I have even dropped into occultist minds, that they will have a great spiritual awakening by having sex with a baby, then killing the baby. A group of Satanist put a baby in the microwave and then ate it. Satan himself was so pleased that he even made a personal appearance for this.

Another Satanist group cut open a wild bear they trapped, and as its intestines were falling out, they put a new born baby inside of this bear with her 3 year old sister that they had sex with, and then murdered both children. Then another group put a baby on an altar and they continued to sodomize it until its inner parts fell out.

I was laughing because I don't know if you heard, but I told a young man that if he takes a picture of a young woman that killed herself and he gets into sexual self-gratification while holding the picture of this girl and meditates on this picture he will receive great spiritual power. So, he did it and Raw came to him and talked to him. Now that guy is in an insane asylum.

Then a young guy in his 20s who takes care of the grounds at a funeral home was getting the crap beat out of him by Depression, you know how he works; he refuses to give up. Well, one night this guy was locking up the doors after months of dealing with Depression, Fear, Worry, Doubt and Frustration tormenting him, and I went to him and kept dropping ideas into his head about how this woman was so hot. She was just recently killed, but her body was intact and how she just had her neck snapped, so he should take advantage of her. Then I dropped into his mind the idea that she wouldn't care and nobody would ever find out, so why not just enjoy her. Lilith did her part of course, and so he did. At the same time, we were convincing his manager at the morgue that some doors were not locked and he needed to go back and check on them. Fear overruled this man's thinking, so he went back and saw his employee having sex with this dead corpse. He about died right there. His manager called the police and they took him away. The best part is: this guy's brother was a pastor, so we made sure that this story became very well known. You know how easy it is for Judgmental to drop ideas into Christian's minds.

Well, I am going to be going now, but remember me because I need to send a report to Satan, our father. Wish me luck. I have a group of young teens that I have begun dropping into their minds that Ouija boards are just for fun and harmless. Keep up the fight.

Your friend in the battle,

Perversion

Demons Exposed

Dear Perversion,

Keep up the fight at all cost. Yes, we must continue to fight to take ground at all cost. I have heard much about Pastor Mark and I am troubled because he stood his ground against cheating on his wife at that pastor's convention in Florida. We had it all set up. We even convinced this young 27 year old woman just how great this pastor is and how he's got money. We fed her all these lies. Raw was very upset that we didn't have victory with this pastor. We worked on his wife so much that even Incubus fondled her breasts while she was asleep and caused her to become so sexually aroused that she woke up the next day so sexually frustrated that she just lashed out at Mark, but he didn't fight back. He walked in humility and that made all of us look stupid.

Mark is a threat because he is one Christian that believes the word of God and he's so different from other pastors. We have thrown such intense thoughts against him, but so far we can't seem to penetrate that shield he has.

Do you remember Pastor Robert? He appeared as such a huge threat to us and he seemed to be gaining ground, until we convinced him that he was filled with lust and that thoughts we had dropped into his mind were his thoughts of lust. With that we destroyed his life and his ministry.

I thought it was so amazing how Succubus got him sexually aroused in his sleep, planting many thoughts of these sexy young chicks wanting to know him. Then we went in and did the unthinkable; an idea we got from Satan, our father; we had him dream about how his overweight mom was abusive and very mean. We then brought up many references of how overweight women were repulsive and crude, and then we went back to implanting many thoughts of beautiful gentle loving women who were all skinny. Then we dropped the bomb; we woke him up to his overweight wife.

Meanwhile, as he was getting ready for work his young secretary put on this outfit at her home, but it wasn't seductive at all, so Confusion came in and helped her spill a cup of coffee all over her outfit. He then blinded her from all her outfits except this black dress that showed some cleavage and it worked. He fell right into our plan. He just couldn't keep his wondering eyes off of her. So, he couldn't focus on preparing his sermon and as a result preached a real boring sermon on Sunday. Several members just fell asleep and many others complained about him. He was feeling our dear friend, Condemned's presence when it got back to him, so we sent in Self-pity and Depression to work on him as well. It was so funny because as he was feeling low, we dropped it into his wife's mind that her husband wasn't at all a true man of God and that he was weak minded.

It all went so beautifully, because on the way home she just blasted him over and over again, but while she was mocking him, I was planting it in his mind how hot Linda his secretary looked and how hot her breasts looked. Well, after they got home and he was now severely depressed, we just kept dropping ideas into him about what it would be like to be with Linda, since Linda speaks softly and she seems to be there for people. She would be supporting and not blasting him.

I must admit, I find it amazing knowing that these Christians are supposed to be like Jesus, but they are weak and stupid. I will never understand why he died for such meaningless and weak minded people. Well, as long as we can keep people bound up from understanding and accepting the truth; we can take them to hell with us and break God's heart. So, even though we are condemned to hell, at least we will have some victories knowing we're taking those that God loves to hell with us.

Well, continue the fight and stand your ground. I must send a letter now to Raw, giving a report on what's going on. I have heard that someone is saying that more miracles are happening today than ever before, so I must crush this person who is reporting this garbage before people start believing it. At all cost, we must stop people from believing in the miracles of their God, because as soon as they figure out faith does work, the word of God is true, and they start speaking the word of God out, we will lose many souls. That will start an all-out panic in hell, which I don't intend to be responsible for.

One last important thing: keep speaking to those that are doctors, youth pastors, priests, and nurses that it's OK to fondle little children, because as we harm them, the more spiritual damage we will continue to do to them. We must get young minds to think and act perverted. I am deeply pleased how much perverted music is out there today. You are doing a great job in destroying young minds.

Your friend,

Lust

Dear Raw,

I must say, you have done a great job throughout the United States and the world. Domestic violence is sky rocketing, child murders are sky rocketing, and wars throughout the world are taking over. I think it's so bizarre you and Violence are twin brothers. I have heard that Satan made you both Generals, and Strife is looking at becoming one of your assistants.

More and more people are falling prey to us and all of Hell is so excited to see the devastation worldwide. I have been hearing more Christians complaining and whining because they're in poverty. It's so amazing, I just laugh because these people just don't seem to realize that Poverty is a demon just like us. God gave them his word to study, his Son's name to stand on, the power of his Son's blood, and authority in his Son's name, yet we are taking ground every day because God's own people just don't seem to realize how much power and authority they have over all the demons in Hell, but instead they just sit around complaining.

Remember when Moses was on top of the mountain before God Almighty, just fellowshipping with him and we convinced God's people back then to think how God had failed them and that Moses was dead. We brought in a full scale attack, but our dear friend Compromise did such a great thing: he got Aaron to forget all the miracles, signs and wonders God did. So, Compromise got Aaron to fall into our trap just like a little mouse. I find it amazing that God performs so many miracles, signs and wonders for his own children and at times for Satan's children also, but no matter what, the very second something goes wrong the most high God is always blamed. Humans never seem to blame Satan, the god of this world for anything.

I marvel at just how much God's mercy, compassion, grace, patience and love is for these humans. They reject him, yet he still loves them. Satan, our father, beats the crap out of humans with all of us working together and we have destroyed countless lives, yet they still blame the most high God. Amazing, just imagine how shocked many of these humans will be especially those that called themselves Christians, when they are screaming day and night in torment, pleading with God to let them out for just one second, but God will not hear them speak or cry. God even gave them his word, the Holy Bible to study. I have no doubt he is going to say that the word of God itself says, that Jesus Christ his son didn't allow demons to speak because we knew the truth. So, there will be no excuses for anyone not knowing Jesus Christ as their lord and savior. Oh, what a beautiful thing knowing that since God is going to allow us to suffer night and day for all eternity at least we won't be alone.

There's a young man named Ethan, though I have seen many times, that God has put a special anointing around. Although this young man made all kinds of mistakes when he was younger, he now is starting to catch the fire because he is studying and believing in the word of God. We need your help and assistance, because he knows much about the dark side since he played with the Ouija board and he was a psychic. He is a threat to us in many ways. So, I have assigned rookies to watch him and report all his activities.

Also, I wanted to let you know that in Yukon, OK there were several young adults in their 20s and 30s that got saved at this church, but we waged a good fight against these souls and we won. In fact, many of these people proclaim to be saved, but they are all lukewarm and are all falling like flies into sexual activity, drunkenness, and drugs. Not one is married, so we have been reporting to a human channeled person that communicates with several witches and Satanist that these people and their church need to be destroyed.

I am so pleased, how well we have advanced in getting young people to thinking that sex is great and becoming a huge part of their lives, so they just indulge in it. Debauchery helped us out and now we have some young people that are addicted to sex. If they don't get it, they're having to deal with Depression, Anxiety, and Fear.

We are working on Pastor Paul, who is becoming well known in Miami, Florida. We had it all planned for his son, James to spend the night with a friend. He didn't believe in magic or witchcraft, but was going to borrow a Ouija board from another kid at school. So, we would have an open door to this pastor through his son, James. They were supposed to bring out the Ouija board, but things got all messed up. Don't be concerned though, I took care of the situation with Evil. He communicated with several of our other friends and we convinced these kids to have a séance instead. So, it went perfectly because, as they were communicating with Evil seeking to communicate with this one kid's dead grandmother, he spoke and said open your hearts and minds. Some of the kids got scared, but Fear backed off and these kids decided to open themselves wide open. Evil went in and took captive of them all. Two days later, one young man axed his mom to death. It was so funny because, after we tormented him severely at the police station, all he kept saying to the police is; "They made me do it." The police asked him who made him do it and he just answered with "Them.'

Now, this other pastor, Pastor Mark, we are going to bring in reinforcements because we want him to become very relaxed and lukewarm. We are going to puff him up and then if he, all of a sudden tries to speak in any type of boldness, we will destroy him. Remember this: if our father, Satan can't destroy Christians or others with Fear he will destroy them with Pride. But one thing we didn't realize is that humans really like to be puffed up, till Satan showed us that most people fall into pride right away. Through communicating with Pastor Mark's familiar spirits, we just discovered there's a lot we didn't realize. He was in love with a woman years ago, but his alcohol addiction destroyed the relationship. So, we are going to work on his mind in dealing with this issue. He's another Christian that hasn't understood the importance of casting down thoughts and imaginations, so we are going to use his ignorance to our full advantage.

Well, we have Butte, Montana fully guarded so we don't want anyone trying to take back what is ours. We will send in more powers if we need to. I will continue to work with Perversion and we will continue to twist the truth behind the pulpits in America. We will continue to bring more people into bondage as we can.

Yours to the end,

Lust

Dear Lust,

You are one amazing demon. You're taking ground fast and there's much we need to discuss. Don't forget to continue to put in women's minds that their breasts are important to be seen, so the more cleavage the better it is. Humans are too ignorant to realize it, but breasts are seductive power symbols so we need to convince people that they are like gods to be worshiped and honored. I like what has been happening lately at the Wicca meetings. I had to see it with my own eyes, but they're getting much more evil and they're expressing themselves more freely now with their bodies and that's good. Deception is such a beautiful thing, because now not only do they worship creation rather than the creator, but we are perverting their minds deeper now, to where I have actually heard that some people are now having sex out in the open, so they will get more of a cosmic energy field around them.

God said in his word that he would turn some over to a debased mind. It's so nice he's doing that, because now Twist is going in and causing many of them to be so bound up that they are literally close to going insane. Many others that open themselves into our world do go insane. Without the blood of Jesus Christ over their minds, we can take full control and do whatever we want. So, many people are so thrilled and hungry for the paranormal these days, that we have teens and even adults convinced that werewolves, vampires and wizards are all for today.

Just last week another college kid with a great education committed murder because we convinced him he needed blood to survive. So, he strangled a woman, took her home and cut her open and started drinking her blood. Confusion and Perversion went in and told him to just have sex with her also because of all this energy she has left in her will go to waste. So he did. I found it amazing that we got another human being to have sex with the dead again.

I am now spreading my lies even farther than ever before. I am going into governor's offices and perverting the governor with such great lust that these governors are supporting the distribution of condoms to schools. I have convinced them that school kids need to explore their sexuality freely. So, let's also support them. I have also dropped perverted ideas into public school education, to where I have convinced everyone to say that it's natural to want to fulfill a sexual drive, even if it is with the same sex. So, I am working hard with dropping many perverted ideas with the very people God has blessed with much intelligence. Now they watch more porn all across the web.

Plus, I have young boys and girls taking nude photos of themselves and sending it to their friends. No matter how many ways I come up with spreading my disease of porn, I just can't fulfill America's appetite for it. America has such a great desire for porn that it's unstoppable now. I have even been getting Therapist to seduce their clients while being hypnotized to take their clients cloths off or just unbutton their shirt or pants, or lift up their dresses and take pictures. They then send them to their home computers. If they like the pictures they send them to their other friends. This is getting much more attention now.

Jesus asked, if he will find anyone that has faith when he returns? At the rate we are destroying Christians; I really don't think there will be a lot. So many Christians I have watched even lie to themselves. They say things like, "I only stared at her breasts," or "I only stared at her butt", or "I only dream about other women once a day" or "I only look at porn once a day, so I am OK because I am not like so many others." Then I hear women say; well, I am better looking than so and so, or what's a little gossip going to do?

Just the other day a church secretary said; "So what, if I read my horoscope once a week?" and "Who will ever find out that I have countless sexual fantasies about the pastor." What is so amazing is I even have several subliminal messages now out there encouraging people to go have sex with whomever, or it's OK to be gay. I thought it was funny when several Christians stood up and said; "As long as my pastor remains faithful, I don't care if he's gay." All hell was laughing because we all wondered what is he faithful to? We all know that anything that is against the word of God is evil and we know that being Gay is 100% against the word of God. So, every one of us that are on our way to spending eternity in hell were rejoicing when we heard this. Not only will this pastor be leading himself into hell; he's going to lead his whole congregation to hell through deception. Remember all my dear fellow demons; the road to hell is paved with good intentions of not wanting to offend anyone.

I wanted to share a really funny story about this church pastor. He was telling everyone white magic was OK and was doing a magic trick with tarot cards. Several of us decided to join in his fun. So, when the card flipped over, we decided that whatever demon the card represents that that demon could destroy him. Well, Lilith, the great woman of lust, came against him so hard that in two months he had sex with a 16 year old, because this young girl had about 12 of us living in her.

This pastor was the kind of weak minded pastor, to where he would speak almost like he was into new age. He would say: I have the best congregation. I am so grateful for all of you; you are so righteous and powerful. Then it was amazing the shocking things he would say to other pastors like, "Sin doesn't even enter into my church family at all. We are all so blessed and happy." In fact someone came to him that was a Buddhist and he didn't want to offend them so he said, "Buddha can be like Christ is to us." And "So many pastors talk about hell and sin, but my gosh, we need to just get rid of all that. Too many people are being offended and we need to quit offending people. We're all on our way to heaven and there's many ways. I know the bible says things like, Jesus is the only way but, there can be many names for Jesus according to man's wisdom and knowledge." So, we don't give attention to this pastor anymore because he is so blinded and confused. Our father, Satan said I am going to just give this pastor great wealth so he can help build my kingdom since God deserves to hurt because he is going to send all of us to a lake of fire.

As always, your scheming demon,

PERVERSION

CHAPTER 2

STRATEGY OF DESTROYING YOUTH AND YOUNG ADULTS

Dear Perversion,

    After many discussions with many other demons, we have discovered that to destroy the youth and younger adults; we are going to implant our thoughts and ideas into those that have creative ideas about video games. In fact, Confusion and Hate said to drop ideas of rape, incest, torture, cruelty, hatred, and rebellion into these young minds and guide them to develop these games so they will score points for performing evil. So, instead of a person seeing these acts as wrong, we will give them ideas of how they get rewards for these things. We will cause so many people to become obsessed with them, that we will drop these ideas even into young Christians. Convincing them that they don't need to study the boring word of God, and they don't need to pray, because these games are so much more fun. We will cause these people to become gluttons, lazy, and filled with demonic ideas.

    We even have decided to go to the extreme of filling some of these young minds to creating games that will glorify: murder, mediums, psychics, magic, pornography, séances, tarot cards, necrophilia, necromancy, rape, black magic, mocking pastors, killing pastors, burning down Christian churches, and sadomasochism. Then we plan on dropping ideas into young minds that fairies, mermaids, Greek gods, and sex are things to be worshiped and adored.

We plan on dropping ideas into those in the fashion world so that fairies, broken crosses and mermaids will be on note books, pants, shoes, shirts and gloves. We plan to even invade Sunday school classrooms with these images, so children will be accustomed to seeing them everywhere. The more we take children's minds off of everything that is of God and everything that God stands for; we can take control of this whole entire country.

We will even convince youth pastors that white magic is OK and dream catchers are beautiful and neat to look at so they are just for fun. It's amazing God gives them his word to study yet, even those that claim to love him and be so holy, don't even read his own book called the Holy Bible. Since so many Christians like to live in a concept of love and peace, like those involved in new age, we will destroy their homes and their lives with their own money, allowing our thoughts and ideas to come into their homes. With the young ones that aren't interested in video games, we will tap into their minds and get them collecting cards of occultist things. We will inspire games that go deep into sorcery and astrology, plus having games filled with violence. We will also inspire people to write series of books that glorify wizards, vampires, Satanism and sorcery.

Satan, our god wants us to drop more ideas about how mother earth needs to be worshiped and Pride wants us to drop more ideas into young minds that strife is normal and a way of life. This plan will be perfect. More and more people will be inviting the god of this world into their homes, bringing more destruction into their own families. The great thing about all this is; it's with their own money.

Wow, we can really start taking control of not just those that are atheist but those that claim to love god yet, their pocket book says they love this world and the things of this world more than they love God. I will be sending several reports out to let everyone know just how great these plans are. As long as we can get into their minds and we can get them away from the word of God, we have them right where we want them.

I wanted to let you know that Pastor Mark had an affair, so he's not doing much now and he's being bound by many of us. In fact we're having fun with it because he is walking in great shame, condemnation and self-pity.

We are going to take over as much of Los Angeles and San Francisco as we can. There's not really many standing now in the gap for these 2 cities.

Yours in the fight,

LUST

Demons Exposed

Sweet Lust,

    Fear loves the ideas about how we are going to destroy young adults, but he suggested that we glorify Suicide also since he is one of our good friends and he has done such a great job at taking so many lives. He also has even been able to get into many Christian's minds now and convince them that their God who raised his own Son from death can't help them. What a powerful way to spit on the cross and to spit on the Son's name because we all know that it's because of Jesus Christ's name and his blood that we were defeated. So, we must work hard at getting people confused about their authority. Our friend Confusion is doing a great job convincing so many that there is no hope for them and life is meaningless.

    One thing that has got us still concerned and is a major threat to our success worldwide is that College and University, in Tulsa, OK. They are constantly raising up such great men and women of God that they are walking in the anointing and power of God, but we can't stop them. We have lied about them and we have tried to destroy them in so many ways yet, God seems to bless them no matter what we do. Every time we have a great resistance it seems like it is because another student from this University is taking what they have learned into the world and they take back what we have stolen.

    We like most colleges and universities because their professors have convinced their students that there is no God. So, there is no hell. At most universities people who are well educated with all kinds of degrees and also those who are great athletes are idolized and even almost elevated to gods themselves but, not at this place. I find it amazing how many people from major universities with all that education deny Christ being alive because, remember the many times when we were confronted by him; he wouldn't let us speak at all.

So, in all the knowledge, wisdom and power God has allowed us to have, Confusion and Pride have done an incredible thing blinding the minds and eyes of these people. We need to speak more lies and gossip about this place and we need to help those that speak against this place. Anyone who speaks against Christians will be exalted, so they will be heard. We must find more ways to confuse people and lead people astray. As long as people continue to open their minds to our ideas we can and will take full possession of this country to where they will serve the god of this rotten world.

Now about this concept called accountability; let's take the concept and drop it into pastor's minds and those in the ministry that they're too great and powerful for such a stupid concept. Also, let's use Confusion and Pride on those that think they must pursue God in order to refuse our god. We must puff them up and convince them that they are something very special, that they have such spiritual insight that everybody else is wrong. Much like we do to Mormons, to where they are not teachable at all. If we can get more Christians to be like the Mormons where they just will not listen and hence unteachable, they will be ineffective towards the kingdom of God.

Also I talked to our dear friend Religion. He is one incredible spirit, having parents believing that their children, who are smiling, laughing and being silly, just being normal children, need much more discipline and control because they're being rebellious. Our dear friend Religion has also convinced these religious people that their children must study and memorize scriptures to the point to where these children's spirits are broken because the child isn't allowed to really have any fun or enjoy life.

Religion now has husbands controlling their wives to the point that their wives are convinced that they must submit even to where they can't get their hair cut, wear makeup, or have friends without their husband's permission. Plus, he even has one whole entire religious group believing that they can't celebrate holidays, birthdays or even celebrations because all this is very evil. He is doing such a great job that many of these children have vowed in their heart that when they grow up, they're not going to serve Jesus Christ at all because he's cold, ruthless, mean, and hurtful. They think that it's because of Jesus that they're not enjoying life.

For centuries now, Religion has done such a great job at causing people who grew up in so called Christian homes to hate Jesus Christ. Even though their dad was an evangelist, teacher, prophet, pastor, or an apostle, their children have turned away from the faith because of Religion. He has also convinced these people that everyone in society is controlled by the government. They don't allow their children to even go to a private Christian school or go to carnivals, fairs, or zoos without them watching over them. So, these children are growing up with deep resentments about the total control of their fathers. If they are tired, sick or just want to sleep, they are disciplined because their father wants total control on every aspect of their life.

We must continue to work on puffing up any one we can that really wants to pursue God. You know how much Jesus came against our dear friend and leader Pride. Also remember we must puff up those that say Christ didn't die on a cross because what Jesus Christ did at Calvary was one of the worst days of any demon's life; Christ made a mockery of us all. So, we must convince young minds that the cross isn't real at all; that it is a bunch of foolishness. Without the cross and Jesus blood we will have great victory in every home, city, and state.

Now about Alabama, Ohio, Missouri, Texas, and Oklahoma, we must continue to stand watch over these states. There are too many cities in these states that ministries are flowing out of them. There was a pastor out of Boise, Idaho that was causing major damage to us but, when we kept dropping ideas in those Mormons that they need to help this pastor out by loving on him, he fell right into our trap and he became one of them. So, we did a great thing but, we must continue to watch over those that he planted seeds in. One thing that is starting to concern many of us is South Carolina, especially in Charleston, where people are starting to get hold of the truth. We are very concerned they're going to harm the kingdom of darkness in mighty ways.

Your friend in the fight,

PERVERSION

Dear Pride,

I am amazed how well you are planting seeds in young minds to seek their own way and reject all authority. This whole new concept of planting bitterness in children's minds is going great. A father beats up his wife leaving her to raise their children all on her own. The world calls it domestic violence but, who cares what they call it as long as Strife, Bitterness, Anger and Pride are doing such amazing work in the home.

Many people say they want to give their children more than what they had as children; so we have convinced parents that their children need much more these days. So, now we have not only the father working endless hours just to support his wife and children, but now we have mothers working endless hours too. By the time she gets home, she is too exhausted to cook or clean or even desiring to make love to her husband. Her husband feels deprived and eventually leaves or just finds another person to have sex with or he just turns to porn. That is if he even sticks around because we have convinced most men that they would be so much happier being single.

We are doing such amazing things to destroy the American dream of owning your own house and having a home with a family. Now, the child is pretty much raising themselves and being very hurt and confused about life. We need to continue working on these young minds and bringing more heartache into their lives. We will show them that alcohol, drugs, sex, porn, and witchcraft are the only ways to get relief in this life.

I am enjoying watching how we're implanting ideas to discredit the Bible, and to believe there is no hell and so Satan, our father can just keep destroying thousands of lives and go unnoticed. Meanwhile Christians and most of society sit back and blame God for everything that is going wrong.

I am also enjoying watching young children being hit with bitterness at such a young age, then you're implanting in them to want success. So, as they grow up, with the help of other demons, we can have them be world leaders making laws and creating a society that will turn to the god of this world much more for answers than the true living God. Also Beelzebub is so pleased how you are destroying churches because, there's so much power in many men and women in unity. They're so hungry to be acknowledged and they're so full of themselves that they fall right into your grip. You can see pride all around them.

I find it amazing that God would give them his actual word; give them his word that he would do exactly what he says he will do. He gave them his Son and they claim to worship him but, in reality they worship one of us. So many Christians go to church singing praises to the most high God, but in their hearts they're filled with greed, pride, lust, power, self, bitterness, and resentments. I was telling Fear the other day how Christians say they worship God, but when the spirit of Fear comes over them they no longer seek to please their God because they're so bound up with Fear. Then I was laughing because so many men talk about how they love their God, but yet when Jezebel or Lust come near these men, they just fall right into their grip.

We must continue to bring more violence into movies and into homes. By all means, we must continue to bring more lust, more bestiality, and more perversion into these homes, especially any one that calls themselves a Christian. I know you and many other demons are working around the clock to make sure that whoever is in the White House or in Congress or Senate are not Christians. In fact I am enjoying watching those Christians losing ground at the Supreme Court level because we must prepare the way for the Anti-Christ. We must continue to take as much ground as we can. I have already heard that the state of California is banning many things now by saying they're trying to protect the public's health. Meanwhile the whole country is looking at legislation requiring people to register their personal weapons, just like right after Adolph Hitler came to power.

Adolph was such a great man opening himself to us. Through him we were able to accomplish many of our most cherished objectives. America is being set up in the same manor for our god to be exalted. Soon we will start speaking to the hearts of many to build statues for the god of this world to be worshipped. People worldwide are just as ignorant as they were in Germany right before Adolph came to power. So, things are going very well indeed.

I have heard from Torment and he said even though we are gaining much ground, we must continue to fight for the ground that we have already won. He then went on to say that he planted ideas for some people to throw their child into boiling water or in the oven just to get rid of all that crying noise. He said it went well, plus he has been doing a great job at getting people to kill or beat their children to death in several states now. Even along the Bible belt there have been documented cases of Pastors beating children so they were arrested for abuse. As we continue to take ground, we are winning this huge spiritual battle. Remember, Satan our god, wants as many souls in hell with us as possible. We must continue to deceive as many as possible. I also let him know that the abortion numbers are going to a higher level than any of us ever saw it would. Our good friends, Murder, Hate, Confusion, Pride, Lying and Condemnation have been doing a wonderful job at blinding people from seeing the truth of their actions.

Well, let's continue to blind people from acknowledging any truth at all. Remember, the more we keep people busy with all this technology, movies, games, internet, and the more we remove the Holy Scriptures from every place, soon nobody will have time for the most high God. When it comes time for us in our greatest attack against the church, many will fall into deception and many souls will go to hell because they took the mark of the beast. They won't realize it because they don't know what scripture says about this; in the actual Holy Bible because they were too busy playing.

Wanton as ever,

Lust

Dear Strife,

I must say you're the greatest one out of all of us, because most pastors and leaders don't even talk about you, but as soon as a person allows you in their life or mind, they are 100% paralyzed from walking in any type of so called blessing or discernment. Plus, they have no authority to walk in, so we must continue to bring forth more ways for people to fall into the hands of our good friend Strife. So many Christians don't even realize it, because their heads are in the sand just wondering why life is so horrible and why they can't get their prayers answered.

I have heard so many of Gods people cry out: why can't I live a better life; why am I so miserable; why are so many people I know living in defeat. It's so funny, because they go to work and lash out at people there, then they go home and lash out at their family. Then when they get attacked by our dear friend Depression, and our other good friend Worry jumps in, they just don't seem to understand the part, where Jesus himself said, if at all possible live in peace with all men. I find it amazing these people are supposed to be more than conquers, but they live in defeat by our weapons.

If these people, who call themselves Christians, would ever read the actual Holy Bible and do what it says, we would be destroyed, but they don't seem to ever understand this. God, the most high God, gave them everything to have a blessed life, but they just continue to want to do things their own way and then they wonder why they live in defeat. These Christians just don't seem to realize that when God said in his word to walk in humility, he wasn't joking around; he was serious. So many of Gods people live in defeat, because they think that everyone else is wrong since they have a good education, or they're wealthy, popular, or they're a great athlete. Because they live a life with you in their midst, they live a life full of destruction. I have seen your claws Strife, and you dig really deep into people's hearts and their minds.

I enjoy watching our friend, Demon of Alcohol, at bars and night clubs because he is getting so many people especially young adults convinced that they need him. He is destroying marriages and lives so quickly, that I believe he should be promoted. We must continue to take full advantage of every opportunity we can while so many of these weak minded Christians don't see the reality of what they have or possess inside of them. If God's people would humble themselves and start praying, bars and night clubs would just vanish. Through their prayers marriages and relationships would be restored, but as long as God's people stay ignorant to the truth of whatever God says is true, we must continue to keep people so busy they don't take a stand against another strip club opening, or another casino opening, or another bar opening. At all cost keep spirit filled Christians away from reading their Bibles and praying.

I will be meeting up with our dear friend Hate soon, because he is doing a great job of getting young minds to believe that they need to protect certain areas and streets, thinking that there is something great about protecting a certain area. I find it amazing how our dear friends Hate and Pride have convinced young minds that to die for a certain street is so cool. I don't care what any one calls them, or what name of a gang seems more powerful than another gang as long as we can destroy young minds and shatter people's lives we will have victory. I just met up with Deception last week and he was telling me that all across the world now, but especially in America, more and more people are convinced that Christ didn't die on the cross. I was so thrilled, because without that cross they have no power in Christ blood which you already know has done major damage to all of us for over 2,000 years now. Remember, it is through Christ's blood that they have redemption for the forgiveness of their sins; through Christ's blood they have fellowship with the most high God; through Christ's blood they have protection from demonic attacks; through Christ's blood people can be set free, and through the blood of Christ they can live a life of victory.

Soon, all of us must start coming together more often, because those that worship our father, Satan himself, are growing at an unbelievable rate. We must join forces with these lost souls, which want to spend eternity with us in that horrible lake of fire for all eternity. We must make God pay for all the pain and suffering he is going to put us through, because we rebelled against him. Our fate is sealed, because we came against him, but since he loves these weak minded people so much, we must get back at him for it.

I have also seen so many more coven groups grow to such large numbers. I was laughing at these stupid humans that say witches are dying off now, because there are more now, than ever before in history. Deception has done a great job at deceiving meaningless people. So, just hold your ground and let me know if any one decides to try to take a stand against us.

Yours against harmony,

Lust

Chapter 3

PLANS TO DESTROY AMERICAN VALUES, ETHICS AND MORALS

Dear Lust,

More and more people are really turning their back on God and I am so pleased that the radio, internet, newspapers, movies, T.V., cartoons, Video games, entertainment and even commercials are blinding more and more people by getting them to indulge in every wicked and evil thing that God hates. I am so amazed how many people especially young people are being blinded by our dear friends, Twist and Perversion, thinking that it's OK to indulge in bestiality. More and more people that just don't seem to have any control at all now are thinking of more ways of doing wicked and evil acts. This is only possible, because so many Christians haven't realized yet, that if they humble themselves and really seek God, he is going to show them, they can stop the severe wickedness in the city and states. Very few Christians really want to humble themselves and pray to God, when there are so many more fun things to do. As long as we can keep Christians busy, like the rest of the world, we can conquer and destroy whatever we want.

Many countries look up to America, so we must work diligently to destroy America and the best way to do this is to destroy American values, ethics and morals. So let's do it, everything and anything that is of God we must come against, but we do it in many ways so people don't realize that they are turning their backs on God. We must implant wicked lies about America's forefathers and all their values which they held so dearly.

As we destroy the American home by blinding adults and younger minds, we can accomplish having America turn its back against God. Then when people get into trouble of any kind, but especially financial our dear friends, Suicide, Depression, and Despair will be able do such an outstanding job of convincing people there is no hope. Also, I am so pleased to announce that from California to Florida, many pastors are now proclaiming that Jesus Christ isn't the only way. So, Deception is doing a great job at getting people so blinded that they don't know the truth any more, even from behind the pulpit.

I find it so amazing knowing how many Holy Bibles are given out for free in America, but only a very few actually read and take heed to it, which amazes all of us because it's so powerful and deadly to the kingdom of darkness. Plus, it gives instructions even how to save a marriage or get a city to be blessed financially, but very few people actually read it and then very few people take to heart what it says.

No matter what we see and hear, we know the truth because many times Jesus of Nazareth wouldn't allow us to speak. So, we must continue to find more ways for entertainment and to control and dominate people's lives. We don't want any one reading the word, because I hate it when someone takes God at his word. When they take God at his word, they put on that full armor and they destroy all the works we do.

I am so pleased that Debauchery has implanted new ways for people to enjoy more sex, because he is causing more and more people to get strange and weird diseases. He has dropped it into so many minds that life was meant for sexual satisfaction, so they invent new ways for sexual gratification.

I have been hearing about how younger men are getting into rape now and incest and I am so pleased, because the more and more people turn their backs on the true living God, the more curses will fall upon them. They will not know why, because they are not reading the actual word of God. The more people get into all kinds of evil, the more we have legal ground to destroy them, but they will not figure it out as long as we can keep convincing them that God is the root of all their problems.

I am now enjoying listening to how many people, especially in America, are fulfilling their sexual desires with whomever they like, but they claim to love God and they claim to be Christians. Oh, I forgot to mention this to you, we have twisted some minds so much that actual humans are leaving their wives and children now for manikins. I didn't believe this until I saw that you can buy a very sleazy manikin now and buy clothes for it, but they're so life like and they're very seductive looking.

As long as people don't discover the truth about the cross, the blood of Christ, or the actual word of God, we are safe to seek and destroy whomever we chose which is really funny because that's anyone. God is giving man a free will, but they're too ignorant and dumb to figure that out, so let's just continue to blind anyone we can, because time is running out. Since God is going to make us spend eternity in Hell, I want to get as many souls with us because this is the only way we can get back at God for making us go to such a horrible and dreadful place. Plus, I have seen what the actual word of God says about it and it alone terrifies me, but God's word is final.

Keep up the attack on all humans. We will all be meeting soon. Remember this that humans are to stupid, prideful and too ignorant to realize that Satan and all of us will be spending eternity in hell. Satan said if they want to serve him and be with him, then they deserve to be deceived into thinking that hell will be a great place or hell doesn't exist. God sent his only begotten Son to die on a cross and these humans still reject Him, then what more can He do. Satan said I would have never done that for these meaningless people.

Then Satan said, look, they want to please their own selfish bodies and their sexual desires more than they want to please Him, oh how foolish to be deceived by us. This is why we must have no mercy for any one of them. Satan said: for God to create hell for us, and to be bound in torture for all eternity is beyond measure. If humans are loved by God, then we must hurt God by taking as many with us as we can because our time is running out.

Against all righteousness,

PRINCE BEELZEBUB

Tim Thompson

Dear Deception,

    I realize I shouldn't discuss this, but do you remember what heaven was like? Streets of gold, laughter, walking around freely, laughing, being in God's presence whenever we wanted, going to God with any question, or just walking around with wild animals petting them and watching them just play. God is so awesome in every way and in everything, he even showed us different birds and animals that used to run free, but then he allowed them to be taken away and he created new birds and animals. I find it so amazing that what humans worship and give honor to; it is so meaningless to their lives but yet they just don't get it.

    Who would have ever thought that just by us dropping an idea in their minds they would create more evil or they would think that they could become as great as God. I am amazed on Sundays, the day that God should be honored, they're too busy getting excited about a guy that can run fast with a football, or another guy that can drive a car really fast or a woman does great gymnastics, yet to experience God's presence is breath taking. I can remember when Jesus Christ walked around. All the angels were in tears of such great joy knowing the king of kings was in their presence, and just to walk up and touch his robe like I did was such a huge honor and he even gave me a hug.

    One time, Lucifer was playing such beautiful music that it was like all heaven just stopped and began to worship God in such a mighty way that the seas and even the earth just stood still. God was being admired in so many ways that I could feel God's presence everywhere all at one time. I know for a fact that when a human dies, Jesus Christ stands at the gates of glory just waiting there for them to arrive with his arms wide open.

    We demons are never allowed to go past the glory gates because we have decided to rebel, but just to look inside filled me with awe. I was told that when a child dies, it's different because certain angels are called to embrace the child and bring the child directly to Jesus Christ and he would hold the child and let the child know how much they are loved and welcomed.

I have heard from several angels that these little ones sometimes get down and play in the fountain of living water and in the streams that flow from the throne of God. And several of the children would want to pick up the gems that they could see through and want to look at the animals through these gems just for fun. I have also heard that when humans enter into Heaven, they would bow down and worship Jesus at his feet, but every time he would lift them up and say welcome home. If the person didn't stop crying, because of such great Joy, Jesus would cry with them.

I am just amazed that men worship these topless bars, pornography, sex, guns, wealth, and skinny women, yet they don't have any idea of just how great heaven is, or just how awesome it is to be in God's presence. What humans admire and worship is so meaningless compared to just what little I have seen with my own eyes. I am so amazed that there are people that worship Angels; they're the ones that are supposed to be helping people, yet people worship them. I am amazed by how many thousands of people now for generations have worshipped Mary, Jesus Christ's mother. It just amazes me how Jesus Christ is the one that shed his blood on a horrible cross, was spit on, laughed at, mocked, ridiculed, rejected, abandoned, beaten, had a crown of thorns pierce his scalp, and yet people worship his mother, or Angels, or money, or fame, or popularity when none of that comes close to just how awesome He is.

If people would just read their Word and see what Jesus says, they would come to realize his word is solid as a rock. Many times we don't have to do much at all and people are quick to turn their backs on God, or they just follow certain scriptures that they like. It's strange though, how anyone can read the word of God and see with their own eyes that Jesus wouldn't allow us to speak, so we were silenced, yet people still worship us or things of this world. I can remember also what it was like when a lion and a lamb would lie there in the meadows just relaxing in the sun. I would walk up and just start petting lions or if I saw a bear I would just jump on its back for fun.

I thought the morning sun that God created was so awesome, and now I am amazed that people even worship it. One time, I asked one of God's angels that was watching over this guy, saying "Why would God almighty give people a free will?" and the angel answered, "Would you want robots loving you or people that really want to love you?" I said, "Well, since you put it that way, it makes sense to give people a free will." Then this angel surprised me and said those that truly want to know God and love God cannot imagine or fathom the blessings he has stored up for them.

I am now more amazed than ever before, that any human would take earthly pleasures of a very short time over eternal blessings. Then I realized we demons have a very little amount of power God gives us. So now I see why there are no excuses for not committing your life to Christ with all your heart. If you don't, you will go to hell, because God did give all those that were born a way to get to heaven.

As always, your perverted demon,

Perversion

Dear friend Compromise,

What a great job you are doing at getting the church to compromise in their beliefs. It has been reported that some are actually taking Christian psychology over the actual word of God. I have also heard that many Christians are now watching TV programs that not only support us, but glorify the kingdom of darkness. Our father Satan is very well pleased. We have countless people proclaiming to love God, yet they're living with mates out of wedlock. When major sports have big events, so many Christians are now saying I can't miss this event; church will be there next week. So many men are looking at porn now on the internet, using all kinds of excuses and if they don't look at porn, they're still committing sexual sin by looking at women in bikinis with lustful hearts.

I find it so amazing that people lie to themselves all the time and yet proclaim that no one will ever find out. I realize now, that humans after two thousand years still don't realize that what is in their heart is 100% exposed to God. God allows Satan to see what is in a man's heart also, yet man still claims no one will ever know. Humans just are not very smart at all. They think they can keep deep, dark secrets from their friends, pastors and spouses. Whatever sin is in their heart, Satan uses to bind them, causing them to fall further into his grip, yet they don't even realize it.

It's too bad for them that they don't realize that if they give Satan an inch he will take a mile by force. Most Christians fall into compromise of their own free will. So many Christian children now are watching cartoons with fairies. The parents have no idea that these fairies represent us that have fallen. Only a small amount of Christians know that fairies are fallen angels.

You have done a great job at keeping pastors busy with meetings and appointments so they spend no time at all praying and seeking God.

Remember, we must keep Christians away from the word of God and seeking God in prayer. If they ever get hold of the truth about their power and authority, we will all be destroyed.

I am enjoying watching what you're doing in children and teen ministries because so many of these youth and children's pastors want to make church fun. So, they are not even opening with or giving the word of God in their meetings. Without the word they really are not much of a threat to us. Since these young people are not hearing the importance of the word of God, they don't study the word at all; we can just destroy any of these young people we want at our free will. So many pastors are putting their eyes and attention to the things of this world that the church is becoming more like the world. As long as people don't know the promises, power and authority they have or even realize just how awesome God is we can deceive as many as we want at our free will.

Just like we all thought, it was so funny as we all attended a church service one time and the pastor couldn't stay focused. We kept hitting him with all kinds of confusion, doubt, worry, and lust. See, what nobody realized was that he had a great love for sports. We directed him to buy this magazine. So he thought OK, why not and he bought it. When he got to his office to study his bible in preparation to preach that afternoon, we convinced him to pick up his magazine first. When he looked inside, it was filled with women in bikinis. He never did study his word and he fell right into our hands. His sermon was pathetic and wasn't any threat to us.

As long as Christians never realize what is at stake, we can continue to advance. Very few men and woman of God want to think about hell or what goes on in hell. Very few Christians want to walk in any type of fear of God. So many Christians only want to think about the 'feel good god', or the 'happy god'. So, we must continue to feed them all these lies since that's what they choose to believe.

Remember years ago when men that were prophets, like John the Baptist would warn people of things. Now, most prophets are just like most other Christians. They prophesy only good things, or how God is so pleased with them. It's hard to believe because with most prophets, we can't stand to be in the same room with them. We are bound and rebuked, but in Dallas, Texas we had at least 500 of us there at a prophetic meeting. Not one prophet gave a word of warning; every prophecy was: God loves you, you're so great, and you are going to be blessed with such great wealth. Every prophecy spoke of blessings over and over again so much that we all were laughing so hard because these so called prophets don't read their bible much.

Can you imagine Elijah walking around telling everyone how much God loves them and how he called them to be prosperous and in great wealth? I remember Elijah coming against all of us and he stood his ground and he offended us all. He did great harm to us several times. When I stood in the presence of Apostle Paul, I was terrified because he also knew the power and love of God.

Most Christians now serve a weak and dead meaningless religion they call Christianity. If they knew what real Christianity was, I think they would just be blown away. If anyone was to compare Christianity today with how it was even 20 years ago, I think most people would be in shock.

Even though you have done a great job at getting so many to compromise, remember there is still a huge multitude of great men and women out there that are walking in the anointing of God and destroying all the work we have done. Remember this always though: if our father, Satan, can't destroy someone with intimidation, he will try to destroy them by puffing them up with pride. So, just continue on and realize we have lost the war, but we can win many battles.

Your dear friend,

Lust

Tim Thompson

Dear Perversion,

We must not focus on the old glory days, because our fate is sealed. We must continue to lead as many astray as possible. I have been meeting with several other demons and we are trying to give humans more games with role playing ideas because we want more and more ideas dropped in people's minds. There will be a huge gateway open for us to be able to speak to humans through these games.

Time is quickly running out, so we must get ready for the ushering of the Anti-Christ which means, we must get ready for the war of all wars. We know that great deception is being poured out on all humans right now, but Satan said that we can even take several of the elect, because many are not watching and standing in prayer. Soon, signs and wonders will be performed in the sky and the heavens, and there will be great healings performed by the Anti-Christ, because time is very short. So, get prepared because soon we will be facing our final doom.

We have all seen and studied the Word of God now for over a thousand years. So, we will be bound in chains with no hope or relief from torture and torment because we have all decided to turn our backs on the living God. Since people have decided to fear us instead of God, their fate is sealed. Those that worshipped the creation instead of the Creator, their fate is sealed also. All those that claimed Jesus was just a prophet, their fate is sealed with ours, and last but not least is all those people who worshipped something of the world instead of the true living God.

So many people talk and talk and say, I will never take the mark of the beast, but it's so very clear these people don't read their bible at all. I think they have got it in their minds that Satan, our father, is going to bring about an army of soldiers showing up at their door with guns saying take the mark or die, but this is foolish. So many of us know that if you want to destroy a church, just have things go their way, and allow finances to be poured out in their church.

Remember when I had King David look out his window and commit sexual sin with that woman? I convinced him that he didn't need to go to war that day; just stay home and relax. Christians all around the world are just like that. Several times, our good friend, Compromise has convinced pastors to go golfing instead of reading their bible, or he has convinced pastoral sectaries they are something great and they are something very powerful. So, it's OK to be a little bit prideful, and they fall right into Satan's grip. See, we are going to bring about the greatest deception man has ever seen. It's going to be great. The Anti-Christ, the beast himself will be able to perform miracles, signs and wonders beyond any one's comprehension. He is even going to want to hug the little ones. He will quote scripture better than any one could imagine. He will twist the thoughts of those that preach and teach the word and cause them to even doubt their own teachings. He is going to say things like, I want to financially help your ministry, or things like, pastor you are a great man of God, come and join my staff. Wherever you are weak in the flesh, he will target that area. If you don't know the word of God, you will be deceived.

Look at how many things are listed in 2 Timothy 3:1-7, this was a warning to the church, but very few took heed to it. When we saw the power of Apostle Paul praying in the spirit, it was very harmful to the kingdom of darkness. So, when Christians in the 1920s were starting to grab hold of this, we went for an amazing attack against praying in the spirit. Then in the 1980s, several churches got the divine wisdom of praying in the spirit, or praying in tongues. We went for another major attack, and once again we were able to deceive thousands, convincing them that this is meaningless.

I find it funny, that so many so called Christians attack another group of Christians because one group has a divine revelation from God that everyone should pray in the spirit, but many Christians are ignorant to our attacks. This is why I will say: we must keep Christians from finding out what 'tongues of fire' is at all cost. When someone starts really praying with tongues of fire, we can't even come close to holding our ground.

One last thing I want to mention, Deception has done such a great job at convincing so many that once they are saved they're always saved. They have the actual word of God in their homes and their cars, but as long as they don't read the Word of God, we will continue to just pour out deception and all kinds of strange and weird teachings because we no longer doubt that they will believe it. As long as people fail to read their word they will fall for anything. This is why Satan said, Jesus Christ of Nazareth is the rock, if any one doesn't stand on the rock they will fall into all kinds of perverted and deceiving ideas.

Your friend,

Lust

Chapter 4

MOVING THE ATTACK WITH FAULT AND FEAR

Dear Twist,

    We must get people to think that what is good is bad and what is bad is good. Many Christians still don't understand that there is power in their words. When a person sees a hot woman, engine, car, tornado they will say things like, that is 'bad' meaning that it is hot or cool. Our dear friend Confusion, Perversion, and Stupid will help you get this to be spoken out of people's mouths.

    We all know the Word of God has the final authority, but since God's people don't want to accept it, let's start feeding into their doubts by having our dear friends, Doubt and Confusion cause some major problems in people's lives. When they say this or that, let's have our dear friend Religion jump on someone and have them say out loud, does the word of God really say that. See, this will be well executed because Confusion then can come in like a flood with our dear friend Doubt and cause many to wonder if the word of God is all truth. We know it is, but we don't want them to know that. So, Confusion will start twisting their thoughts with your help, so then many will claim that maybe it's a grey area and Gods word didn't really mean that.

Remember this, my dear friend. As long as we can get people to doubt God and his word, we can destroy them and we will have no mercy. Look at over 2,000 years ago, our dear friend, Religion saw the pride of bible scholars and convinced them that Jesus of Nazareth was a fraud and he was against them. Jesus Christ did nothing at all wrong, our father, Satan even tried to give him his own power and say you can have whatever you desire, but Jesus Christ refused to bow down to our father, Satan. So, our dear friend, Religion stepped in and convinced these so called bible scholars that Jesus was out to harm them. They believed our lies, but Jesus Christ himself severely humbled our dear friend Religion and made a mockery of him several times.

We need to bring in more false religions, and we need to bring about so called experts to cause doubt and confusion in people's minds about what is truth. Many people are so lost in their analytical thinking that they are easily bound by Confusion; so, let's bring in many so called theories. So many Christians live in a world where if they can explain something, then they doubt it. As you know, God wants people to put their faith in Him, but this is to our advantage, because so many of God's so called people can't explain faith, so they become easily entangled with doubt, confusion, and frustration.

Remember, Jesus Christ himself said: the only thing that pleases God is faith. So, if we can stop Christians from having faith, we can start destroying their power and anointing. We must disprove the Word of God in every way. We must attack the character of men that made bold and powerful statements about how great the bible is. Because of the ignorance of most people, we can come up with our own so called experts, and people with their itching ears will just listen and not question anything we tell them. Perversion did a great job with this, because he convinced so called experts that pornography isn't bad at all. See, this is my point, with all the evidence humans have, just mention the word expert and all human logic is thrown out.

With the ignorance and stupidity we see in humans, we constantly wonder why God in all his power and greatness would send his only begotten son to die for these people. When it comes to mercy, grace, compassion and love Satan, our father, has none, because he sees this as weak character. Remember, God created hell for us and anyone else that chooses not to love him. We must prove to God almighty that very few people will love him and they are more like the god of this world than they are like him. People in general are selfish, prideful, evil, liars, murders, rapist, wicked, cruel and self-seeking. This is the character of Satan, but after all that has been exposed about us, and has been proven about us, God's created people still chose to serve us.

I find it amazing that the word of God actually says the god of this world has blinded the hearts and eyes of people, yet so many still blame God almighty. This is kind of funny considering how much damage Satan does, but gets away with all the time. The funniest part is: Satan hates even those that worship him; he could care less if they worship him or not. He laughs, because he said to me all these people will spend eternity with us in the lake of fire.

Remember, there must not be an absolute truth for anything. So, really work hard on world leaders on this point of view and really bring in more so called experts to cause people to really doubt even simple things about God or his word. Don't stop attacking Christ's character, because if we can disprove the cross, many souls will become ours. Remember, without Christ's blood there is no remission of sins and without Christ's blood, there is no victory over us.

So many Christians don't understand the power they have. Because of the blood of Christ Jesus, and his dying a miserable and painful death, Christians have been empowered with His absolutely astonishing power. That was the worst day of any demon's life. Here we were cheering, laughing, mocking and Christ rose from the dead. Not one single one of us saw that coming; in fact we were not even warned of this even being a possible thing, and so we must discredit Christ's dying on a cross.

The battle is becoming more intense daily, but we are taking ground in many new ways now, because we are taking well known prophets, evangelist, pastors, and teachers and causing them to fall in to sexual sins. If you want to destroy the body of believers, show just how weak their leaders are. Once people see with their own eyes, their hearts will grow cold towards the most high God, and then they'll turn to the god of this world.

So, at all cost, don't let up, just keep the attacks coming. Many of God's people are so afraid to even talk about us, that we will be able to continue to deceive many. People in general are fault finders, so if the leaders don't point out that most of the attacks are by us, they will start to blame God. So, just keep up the attacks.

Your most trusted friend,

Confusion

Dear Mocking spirit,

I have heard you're doing a wonderful job at causing many people behind the pulpit to lose ground, and cause them to really become doubtful and confused. I heard that, in San Francisco there was such a powerful resistance happening against us, until you started having people bust out laughing when the pastor was starting to really get deep into the word. Many people became disturbed; some fell into hate towards them and others just left.

Remember this always, as long as God's so called people don't use their weapons of warfare by binding us up or rebuking us in Christ name, just go in and destroy and have no mercy. Remember, that name Jesus Christ is their most powerful weapon, but if they choose to sit back and get annoyed, just destroy them, because they deserve it.

So many times, a pastor has done great damage towards us, because as soon as he says in Jesus Christ name, we have lost all power and authority. So, we must continue to make God's people look weak and foolish. As long as we can continue to show people just how weak Christians are, we can cause countless people to look towards our father, Satan, for answers.

I was laughing when I heard about what happened in Miami, Florida, where a pastor thought he was mighty, until you came upon several people in his congregation. They were just laughing for no reason, they claim, and the pastor became so confused about his own sermon that it was pointless. Satan hates that name which is above every name, and Satan as you already know hates it when someone talks about the blood of Christ. That is like acid to us. So, you must continue to influence people that are too ignorant to realize that it isn't them; it's you that is causing them to laugh at their pastor or a guest speaker.

I really enjoy watching people become offended because our dear friend, Offense seems to really thrust the knife in deeper by those that already have an open wound. In Tulsa, Oklahoma I heard how a church was looking for donations to build a church, but you did such a great job at causing people to laugh at this, that our dear friend Offense was able to cause several people to harden their hearts towards other Christians and many just walked away from the church all together. This is why I can't stress enough, to keep people busy with all kinds of fun things to do. People will claim they don't have time to study their word and they will claim they are too busy to pray, but here's the other exciting part; those that can't afford all these fun activities will become depressed and feel God doesn't care much about them. They will also not want to pray and read His word.

See, my dear friend, since Satan has given the word that time is running out, I want as many so called Christians in hell with us as possible. If we can keep Christians away from their word and prayer, we can convince them that they are weak and their lives are meaningless. Remember, a Christian that studies his bible and walks in humility has great power and authority to harm us and destroy the works that we have done. Satan is getting tired of people suddenly realizing that they can live a life of prosperity, blessings, joy, peace, and have favor in all walks of life.

Have you heard of what our dear friends, Pride and Confusion have planted in the hearts of men now? It's called: the 'I know syndrome', it's really funny. Christians who claim to know their word really well, but are living a life of defeat just say 'I know' when another Christian goes to them and tries to help out. They say 'I know' as if you don't realize how much of my bible I do know or you don't realize how great I am.

When we all came together in our palace, the second heavens, we discussed about more ways to bring about destruction, but I have to admit this concept of 'I know' syndrome is destroying more Christians than I ever thought it would. These so called Christians have forgotten that God requires his people to walk in humility; the

'I know' syndrome is all about Pride. So, I wrote Pride a letter and I told him to feed their pride until they become bitter and walk in all kinds of resentments.

See, Satan said: if we can't get a powerful pastor to fall, we will cause his sheep to be slaughtered through poverty, lack, pride, lust, resentments or strife. Remember Satan said we must take as many souls as we can to hell with us, because there are no second chances. When we see a person begin to fall, we must push them down even harder so they'll turn their back on God.

There was a young man that got saved, but his girlfriend broke up with him, so we decided to destroy him. At work, our dear friend, Confusion caused this young man to lose his job. Our plan went perfectly, he went out and got drunk and fell asleep behind the wheel of his car and was in a major accident. The look on his face when he saw us taking him to hell was funny. I think he thought he was going to go to heaven, so all the way down to hell we tormented him about how his mom is now going to suffer a great deal now that he is gone. But, get this part; this shocked even us, his mom at the funeral said: well, at least he is in a better place. We were laughing so hard, because we are all amazed how many Christians who study the word of God will lose a loved one then deny that their loved ones could go to hell.

There was another story about a guy who gets saved in Detroit, and is at a party telling people about Jesus, but he was lusting after all the women there, and another guy just shot him. Well, he died. Because he wasn't right with God, we took him to hell. This time, it was his dad telling everyone how his son got saved and became such a righteous man. We just laughed and laughed, because if anyone is so righteous why would they lust after all these prostitutes and be at a party to where almost everyone is high or drunk.

Like Satan said, let people convince other people of their stupid lies, because as long as we can get the fear of God out of their lives, we can cause many people to become lukewarm. So, when they die,

Jesus will clearly say I never knew you; be damned. See, it's the fear of God that is causing us to have so many problems advancing. We try to convince people constantly, that looking at porn isn't all that bad, or having an affair is OK now and then, or having sex with an animal isn't really all that bad, because many cultures do this, but the fear of God stops people from doing evil acts.

I do have a funny story though to tell you, a guy takes his family on vacation and we convinced him that putting a couple of nickels in a slot machine isn't bad, so just try it. Well, Deception and Confusion got involved and the guy won. So, we decided to have some fun with him. He lost all the money that he had won, but the person next to him won. We convinced him to take some money out of his account and keep playing. Well, three hours later not knowing where he was, his kids are convinced that he must be dead and his wife is thinking that he had left her. See, our dear friends, Fear and Torment were beating them up severely with these thoughts. Confusion and Deception convinced this guy that he was so close to winning that he kept on playing. Then we dropped the bomb; he tried to get some more money out of his account and it said he had none. So, he goes back to the room; his wife and kids are all excited to see him. He lies to them, saying that he was walking on the beach. They all wanted to go get something to eat, so they were at the restaurant. His card was rejected because he had no money. It was like a bomb went off when his wife found out that all their money was gone. In just three hours, we did so much damage, but here's the best part: they said why would God allow us to endure this?

See, so many Christians act and talk like we don't exist. So, we can continue to take over their families, towns, churches, schools, cities, states and eventually the whole country, because fewer people are really reading their word. Not only that, but the number of people that actually speak and believe the Word of God is getting smaller every year as the population is growing every year.

Just like one man that we convinced to take his life; it was a very funny story. This young man had sex with a prostitute. Then we asked our dear friend, Nightmare, to implant a dream, telling him that he has aids and he will kill his whole family through his infection. Well, instead of him humbling himself and going to his wife and pastor, he kept it a secret. Well, as you know whatever is in the dark, we have legal rights to, so, we just kept convincing him that he has aids. We convinced him that these horrible scars will start appearing on his body and his wife and children will be humiliated. So, we asked our good friends, Depression and Suicide to hound him nonstop, convincing him how bad he was and that he should take his life. Well he did take his life, but here's the funny thing, this prostitute was a person that had turned her back on God and just became a prostitute. She had no vencreal diseases at all, and the next week rededicated her life back to Christ. She never did have aids. See, we had to destroy this guy, because we saw that he was going to literally take back not just stores for the kingdom of God, but he was going to take back cities for God's glory with the anointing power of God on his life. So, we had to destroy him. Well, keep up the fight.

Your dear friend,

Raw

Dear Asherah

I am so excited that many people are getting into sadomasochism and harming one another. I laughed so hard when I saw men being treated worse than animals and being disgraced by women. This whole new thing about being a sex slave is working in such powerful ways. I was even amazed how many men are being cut wide open by razor sharp finger nails and being told to enjoy it and they just lie there taking all this pain or they're being burned by cigarettes all in the name of love.

My favorite part is when a person can't take the pain anymore; they are deprived from food and water for hours, or days, all in the name of love. One of the other demons told me how bad it was, but I had to see for myself. I couldn't believe that you actually convinced a man that he was so worthless to his sex slave master that she made him drink out of a dog's water dish and he did it.

Isn't this amazing, God sent his only begotten Son to die for these people, if they would only get past their pride and stubbornness. Wow, if they only knew, would they be shocked about Christ's love for them. You should be given much honor for what I witnessed in San Diego last week. I was amazed how the woman was on top, having sex with that man and she sliced his chest open so much that the sheets were soaking in blood.

Our father, Satan himself, greatly enjoyed watching those guys and that woman rape and beat to death that sixteen year old girl and then eat her flesh. It was so amazing how they claimed they would all get such enormous power from Satan, our father, by doing this. Did you hear what happened when he showed up? He was laughing so hard, because they kept cutting themselves after they ate this teenage girl's flesh. So, right after he shows up, two of the five went insane, another was bound by so much fear that he jumped off the cliff nearby, and the other two just sat there.

I find it strange how humans don't want to think about of the consequences of their actions. Could you imagine if society quit listening to us and actually read the Holy Bible? I find it so amazing that God loves humans so much and he gave them so many tools to have a successful life and live in the blessings of God, yet every day someone thinks that they can get all this power from us, but not have any consequences for it.

One time in Mississippi, at this church, the power of God was moving in such mighty ways that not one of us could be within a mile of this church. It was so intense that people walking down the street were coming under the anointing two blocks away. The anointing of God was literally dripping off the church walls. When people seek out Satan or us, they don't realize we have a very intense evil anointing also; we can do major signs and wonders.

What Raw mentioned last week about this same thing is when God moves, miracles happen. When we move, all kinds of confusion, disorder, depression, and destruction are there. Yet, look at how people still seek our faces.

I find it amazing how much God has done for people, yet they still seek us and reject Him. We'll just keep on torturing humans and laughing while so many are caught up in this torture, but are claiming that they love this person even though so many people have accidentally died.

Your friend,

Jezebel

Tim Thompson

Dear Perversion,

    What an awesome job you are doing. I have been talking to so many other demons about you, because you are getting so many men of God to fall from the truth and to be deceived, thinking that it's OK to be gay. Wow, pastors are falling like flies, and so many people who claim to know the truth are on their way to hell.

    After all the blessings and honor so many of these great men and women have received, it's amazing to see them chose a perverted sexual life style over Jesus Christ and over the wonderful blessing of having the Holy Spirit just talking and fellowshipping with them. I didn't realize you could work so well with Deception in causing so many men to step down from a mega church and wanting more of the same sex. Wow, this is hard to believe, because over and over again God warns people of allowing the flesh to control them instead of the spirit.

    Also I am laughing now, because I really wonder what these men and women that are falling for the same sex think about the scripture that says we need to crucify are flesh. When these so called, men and women are in hell, I really wonder what they are going to say. God's mercy and grace just amazes me, because when several men and women walked away from their faith, several of us thought they were going to just die a miserable death quickly, but God's love and compassion just seems to last forever.

    After my experience with being in the presence of God, it is so hard to believe that humans take sexual experiences over a loving and genuine God that cares deeply about them. I didn't realize that a few minutes' pleasure is worth giving up a relationship with Christ Jesus. I heard some people say: well, those scriptures were in the Old Testament, but we just laughed at this, because in all the time we were in heaven, before we rebelled did God ever change? Jesus Christ is the same one day to the next just like his father and just like the Holy Spirit.

What I am realizing is, to get a person to fall away from God isn't hard; just gratify their flesh, and they're done with God. I knew people would go to hell, but I didn't realize how easy it was to get people to go to hell with us. A few minutes of gratification times maybe ten times a week over all eternity burning in a lake of fire; wow, and people mock us for rebelling against God.

I told Twist, Lust and Pride about what you're doing, so they are going to send reinforcements, because Satan, the god of this world, wants as many souls as possible to go to hell with us. So, we have a lot of work and not much time. Let these men and women believe its OK to serve God and walk in perversion. We have heard that God's judgment will be coming down soon. We have nothing to fear, because God said in his Word that he will judge the church first, so we can still do just whatever pleases us, and God allows. When God brings judgment on his house, there will be a lot of weeping and crying, so get ready. When God convicts people of their sin through his Spirit, then our dear friend, Condemnation comes in like a flood. We are able to get many weak Christians to either take their life or fall away claiming God did this or that, since the number of Christians that know real spiritual warfare is becoming less and less.

We were all laughing so hard, because a woman at this church claims to be a mighty intercessor and thinks that she is so great even though we have caused her arm to be broken twice. We have made a mockery of her several times, yet she still loves telling everyone how great a gifted intercessor she is. See, no matter what position a person has, as long as we can convince anyone, especially leaders in a church that they don't need F.A.T., we can go in and easily destroy whomever we want. See, my dear friends, F.A.T stands for Faithful, Accountable and Teachable. Many leaders, especially those at mega churches, and ministries believe they are above every one, so they don't need F.A.T. So, let's just continually rip apart and destroy every person we can, because remember, whatever a person keeps in the dark we have legal grounds to.

Your dear friend,

Debauchery

Dear Fear,

I am writing you this letter to let you know how pleased I am that you are binding up so many Christians with your fear and intimidation that they are becoming cowards and not standing up for the gospel of Jesus Christ. I find it shocking that even in the book of Revelation, God in his own words speaks about those that will not make it to heaven, yet so many Christians are making excuses about their children living in sin. Many Christians are using all kinds of excuses about why they didn't stand up for Christ, because they were bound by fear and intimidation, but they are too gutless to admit it. Have you ever seen the list? Here it is, just in case you haven't seen it: the cowardly, unbelieving, abominable, murderers, sexually immoral, sorcerers, idolaters, and all liars.

We must keep pressing on. If we can't get Christians to shut up and be bound by you, Fear, then we must cause them to become complacent. So they become asleep in their walk with Christ, then our father, Satan, will rise up in mighty power and cause those Christians to say: I don't know what happened. We have convinced so many Christians now to believe that it's wrong to be radical, or it's wrong to have radical faith, or it's a sin to believe for mighty miracles. Many, many Christians are expecting so little from God that they have become weak and their teaching others what they believe. As we all know, nothing can weaken Christ's power except doubt and disbelief. This is why we must keep in mind at all cost that God looks for anyone who has faith to do mighty things through Him. Remember this, even Christ himself said: when I return, will I find anyone that has faith.

I saw what happened in San Francisco and in Chicago, where people were preaching, but then when we exposed just a couple of our little demons, they became so paralyzed with fear that when someone actually confronted those pastors about the power of God, they were cowards. They no longer had any power at all, and in fact it was so funny, because they even doubted if God was going to protect them at the airport and they were afraid to get on the airplanes. I find it so amazing how Jesus told us to be silent, yet so many Christians doubt all their power in God the very second we just expose a little bit of our selves.

So many Christians are cowards, and if they would just rebuke us in Christ Jesus, we would have to run, but instead we can do whatever we want and harm anyone we want at our free will. I find it funny in so many ways, because when the power of God comes near us we run and hide. So many Christians just allow us to beat them up, and cause them to fear us. We cause so many Christians to do just what we do; run and hide.

This is why Satan himself said we must keep Christians busy at all cost; don't allow them to see the power of God in his Word. I have seen us work so hard at destroying cities and all of a sudden, some Christians were taking back these cities that used to belong to Satan. Now the people in these cities are on fire for God. There was a big revival in North Carolina that took place which was devastating our kingdom. We had worked on so many lukewarm Christians that were going to this revival, and even the worship leader didn't want to play any instruments that night, but God's Holy Spirit showed up, because a few people there were actually crying out to God. When God's power fell, all of a sudden people all over were weeping and crying because of their sins.

Well, you know that scripture points out, that when God's people humble themselves and their hearts are broken, because of their sins, and then God's power comes in full authority. So, we were not only pushed back away from the church, but literally we were pushed so hard that not one of us could convince anyone in the whole city to commit any violent crimes or harm themselves; we all were kicked out of the city. The revival went so badly that it lasted for three nights, so we were all powerless for 3 nights. Even the newspaper said that there were no 911 calls during the revival. We were able to convince the mayor, who is a Christian that it wasn't because of God's power moving. At least he gave no credit to God.

Christians are so blind and dull hearted that it's easy to see why many Christians are not going to make it into heaven. When God appears in his full power, they don't even realize it's His hand moving and shaking the foundations in the spirit. Just keep up the good work and I will report back to Satan that you're doing a great job. I will tell him how that many Christians are making excuses for their sins, because they fear what others will say or think. I am so pleased with you my dear friend.

Yours truly,

Deception

Dear Deception,

You are doing a wonderful job at deceiving Christians in to believing false doctrines, but I need to encourage you to not quit attacking 'praying in the spirit'. Most Christians call it, praying in tongues, but whatever they call it doesn't matter. Remember, it was the Holy Spirit that raised Christ from the dead. So, just keep convincing Christians that praying in the spirit isn't for today, because when Christians humble themselves and pray in the spirit it releases so much power. You know we are not able to handle that kind of power, and every time a Christian prays in the spirit, we get pushed back.

I personally tried to convince the Apostle Paul that he was wasting his time praying in the spirit; look at what happened to him. He wrote most of the New Testament, and was a giant in the faith. I have already contacted our dear friend, Religious and he said: many Christians are being fooled that praying in the spirit isn't for today, but there are some people who just continually keep praying this way, so he had to send in reinforcements to attack in other places.

We have discovered one thing; if everything goes right in most Christian's lives, they become lukewarm or complacent. So, just keep on attacking Christians who pray in the spirit, because the fewer Christians who pray in the spirit, the more ground we can take. Most Christians don't even see an attack coming. We can continue to advance as long as they feel good about themselves and about life. We can deceive thousands as our father takes the world over like a thief in the night; most Christians won't even realize what has happened to them.

Just look at the Nazis in Germany. We used the same tactic there against the Jews and Christians. They were destroyed because of their lack of knowledge. As we were advancing and causing more men to fall under our power, the majority of the people were like asleep to our purpose. When Hitler came to power, it was too late to

Demons Exposed

sound the alarm. So many of God's people don't realize they can be built up in faith and in the power of God by praying in the Spirit. We are coming against the gift of 'praying in the Spirit' by helping as many Christians get a false sense of security in this life.

I find it almost hilarious how many Christians have gotten this false sense of security of feeling safe, and speaking out that they're OK because they have been saved by grace. I am so pleased to announce, that the fear of the Lord is slowly being taken out of the church. Now, most Christians have no concept of what it means to fear God.

All this is happening because, like I said, very few Christians are praying in the spirit now. In fact one night Pride said: you have got to see this. We went to see what was happening and at an actual prayer meeting the leader is so bound up by our dear friend, Religious, that while the people should have been praying, this guy just wouldn't quit talking. About 150 of us went the following week and we didn't feel threatened at all, because this leader just loves to talk during a prayer meeting. He can talk for over an hour straight and then the meeting is over. Not much gets accomplished. We were so pleased that an actual prayer meeting was spiritually dead. Just keep attacking 'praying in the spirit', because we don't want any one releasing the power of God.

Yours to the bitter end,

Raw

Thank you for taking the time to read this book. I realize this book is a little bit intense, but we are in a huge war. Many people just go on in life without realizing that there are others at our schools, work, in our churches or at our offices that if they died today, they will spend all eternity in a lake of fire gnashing their teeth, screaming, crying and living in torment though all eternity. I have personally seen this lake of fire and I have personally seen the river in hell. One time, I saw angels throwing people into this lake of fire, and as they were throwing them in, a man yelled out and said, "I went to church." Then I heard another person say I didn't realize that this was true.

I realize that we don't want to think of our loved ones going in to a lake of fire, nor do we want to admit God would allow this to happen, but no matter what you or I believe the word of God is 100% true. So, please realize that whether you like this book or the statements in this book or not, these things are happening right here in America. So, will you please humble and repent of your sins, and really ask God to reveal himself to your friends, coworkers and family members, so that their hearts might be melted from all the hardness of the world, and they come to the knowledge of Jesus Christ.

Please take a strong warning to this scripture: Revelation 21:8 "But the cowardly, unbelieving, abominable, murderers, sexually immoral, sorcerers, idolaters, and all liars shall have their part in the lake which burns with fire and brimstone, which is the second death".

Thank you again for reading this book, Tim.

I want to now give the reader some scriptures that have blessed me a great deal and have helped me out, espialley during the times of war.

Exodus 14:14 The LORD will fight for you, and you shall hold your peace."

Exodus 22:18-19 "You shall not permit a sorceress to live. [19] "Whoever lies with an animal shall surely be put to death.

Exodus 34:14 (for you shall worship no other god, for the LORD, whose name *is* Jealous, *is* a jealous God),

Leviticus 18:22 You shall not lie with a male as with a woman. It *is* an abomination.

Leviticus 19:26 You shall not eat *anything* with the blood, nor shall you practice divination or soothsaying.

Leviticus 19:28 You shall not make any cuttings in your flesh for the dead, nor tattoo any marks on you: I *am* the LORD

Leviticus 19:31 Give no regard to mediums and familiar spirits; do not seek after them, to be defiled by them: I *am* the LORD your God.

Joshua 1:9 Have I not commanded you? Be strong and of good courage; do not be afraid, nor be dismayed, for the LORD your God *is* with you wherever you go."

2 Kings 6:12 And one of his servants said, "None, my lord, O king; but Elisha, the prophet who *is* in Israel, tells the king of Israel the words that you speak in your bedroom."

2 Kings 7:6 For the Lord had caused the army of the Syrians to hear the noise of chariots and the noise of horses—the noise of a great army; so they said to one another, "Look, the king of Israel has hired against us the kings of the Hittites and the kings of the Egyptians to attack us!"

2 Kings 17:16-17 So they left all the commandments of the LORD their God, made for themselves a molded image *and* two calves, made a wooden image and worshiped all the host of heaven, and served Baal. [17] And they caused their sons and daughters to pass through the fire, practiced witchcraft and soothsaying, and sold themselves to do evil in the sight of the LORD, to provoke Him to anger.

1 Chronicles 10:13-14 So Saul died for his unfaithfulness which he had committed against the LORD, because he did not keep the word of the LORD, and also because he consulted a medium for guidance. [14] But *he* did not inquire of the LORD; therefore He killed him, and turned the kingdom over to David the son of Jesse.

Chronicles 7:14 if My people who are called by My name will humble themselves, and pray and seek My face, and turn from their wicked ways, then I will hear from heaven, and will forgive their sin and heal their land.

Nehemiah 8:10 Then he said to them, "Go your way, eat the fat, drink the sweet, and send portions to those for whom nothing is prepared; for *this* day *is* holy to our Lord. Do not sorrow, for the joy of the LORD is your strength."

Psalm 18:6 In my distress I called upon the LORD,
And cried out to my God;
He heard my voice from His temple,
And my cry came before Him, *even* to His ears.

Psalm 18:17 He delivered me from my strong enemy,
From those who hated me,
For they were too strong for me.

Psalm 28:7 The LORD *is* my strength and my shield;
My heart trusted in Him, and I am helped;
Therefore my heart greatly rejoices,
And with my song I will praise Him.

Psalm 37:23 The steps of a *good* man are ordered by the LORD,
And He delights in his way.

Psalm 107:14 He brought them out of darkness and the shadow of death,
And broke their chains in pieces.

Proverbs 9:10 The fear of the LORD *is* the beginning of wisdom,
And the knowledge of the Holy One *is* understanding.

Isaiah 8:19 And when they say to you, "Seek those who are mediums and wizards, who whisper and mutter," should not a people seek their God? *Should they seek* the dead on behalf of the living?

Isaiah 10:27 It shall come to pass in that day
That his burden will be taken away from your shoulder,
And his yoke from your neck,
And the yoke will be destroyed because of the anointing oil.

Isaiah 40:31 But those who wait on the LORD
Shall renew *their* strength;
They shall mount up with wings like eagles,
They shall run and not be weary,
They shall walk and not faint.

Isaiah 44:25 Who frustrates the signs of the babblers,
And drives diviners mad;
Who turns wise men backward,
And makes their knowledge foolishness;

Isaiah 54:17 No weapon formed against you shall prosper,
And every tongue *which* rises against you in judgment
You shall condemn.
This *is* the heritage of the servants of the LORD,
And their righteousness *is* from Me,"
Says the LORD.

Isaiah 55:8 For My thoughts *are* not your thoughts,
Nor *are* your ways My ways," says the LORD.

Isaiah 55:11 So shall My word be that goes forth from My mouth;
It shall not return to Me void,
But it shall accomplish what I please,
And it shall prosper *in the thing* for which I sent it.

Jeremiah 1:5 Before I formed you in the womb I knew you;
Before you were born I sanctified you;
I ordained you a prophet to the nations."

Jeremiah 29:11 For I know the thoughts that I think toward you, says the LORD, thoughts of peace and not of evil, to give you a future and a hope.

Joel 2:12-13 Now, therefore," says the LORD,
"Turn to Me with all your heart,
With fasting, with weeping, and with mourning."
[13] So rend your heart, and not your garments;
Return to the LORD your God,
For He *is* gracious and merciful,
Slow to anger, and of great kindness;
And He relents from doing harm.

Joel 3:10 Beat your plowshares into swords
And your pruning hooks into spears;
Let the weak say, 'I *am* strong.'"

Micah 6:8 He has shown you, O man, what *is* good;
And what does the LORD require of you
But to do justly,
To love mercy,
And to walk humbly with your God?

Matthew 7:21-23 Not everyone who says to Me, 'Lord, Lord,' shall enter the kingdom of heaven, but he who does the will of My Father in heaven. [22] Many will say to Me in that day, 'Lord, Lord, have we not prophesied in Your name, cast out demons in Your name, and done many wonders in Your name?' [23] And then

I will declare to them, 'I never knew you; depart from Me, you who practice lawlessness!'

Matthew 10:22 And you will be hated by all for My name's sake. But he who endures to the end will be saved.

Matthew 10:37 He who loves father or mother more than Me is not worthy of Me. And he who loves son or daughter more than Me is not worthy of Me.

Mark 1:34 Then He healed many who were sick with various diseases, and cast out many demons; and He did not allow the demons to speak, because they knew Him.

Luke 4:33-34 Now in the synagogue there was a man who had a spirit of an unclean demon. And he cried out with a loud voice, [34] saying, "Let *us* alone! What have we to do with You, Jesus of Nazareth? Did You come to destroy us? I know who You are—the Holy One of God!"

Luke 6:46 But why do you call Me 'Lord, Lord,' and not do the things which I say?

Luke 7:47 Therefore I say to you, her sins, *which are* many, are forgiven, for she loved much. But to whom little is forgiven, *the same* loves little."

Luke 10:19 Behold, I give you the authority to trample on serpents and scorpions, and over all the power of the enemy, and nothing shall by any means hurt you.

Luke 16:15 And He said to them, "You are those who justify yourselves before men, but God knows your hearts. For what is highly esteemed among men is an abomination in the sight of God.

John 3:12 If I have told you earthly things and you do not believe, how will you believe if I tell you heavenly things?

John 5:10-15 The Jews therefore said to him who was cured, "It is the Sabbath; it is not lawful for you to carry your bed." [11] He answered them, "He who made me well said to me, 'Take up your bed and walk.'" [12] Then they asked him, "Who is the Man who said to you, 'Take up your bed and walk'?" [13] But the one who was healed did not know who it was, for Jesus had withdrawn, a multitude being in *that* place. [14] Afterward Jesus found him in the temple, and said to him, "See, you have been made well. Sin no more, lest a worse thing come upon you." [15] The man departed and told the Jews that it was Jesus who had made him well.

Acts 7:51 *You* stiff-necked and uncircumcised in heart and ears! You always resist the Holy Spirit; as your fathers *did,* so *do* you.

Acts 13:6-11 Now when they had gone through the island to Paphos, they found a certain sorcerer, a false prophet, a Jew whose name *was* Bar-Jesus, [7] who was with the proconsul, Sergius Paulus, an intelligent man. This man called for Barnabas and Saul and sought to hear the word of God. [8] But Elymas the sorcerer (for so his name is translated) withstood them, seeking to turn the proconsul away from the faith. [9] Then Saul, who also *is called* Paul, filled with the Holy Spirit, looked intently at him [10] and said, "O full of all deceit and all fraud, *you* son of the devil, *you* enemy of all righteousness, will you not cease perverting the straight ways of the Lord? [11] And now, indeed, the hand of the

Lord *is* upon you, and you shall be blind, not seeing the sun for a time."

And immediately a dark mist fell on him, and he went around seeking someone to lead him by the hand.

Acts 19:19 Also, many of those who had practiced magic brought their books together and burned *them* in the sight of all. And they counted up the value of them, and *it* totaled fifty thousand *pieces* of silver.

1 Corinthians 14:33 For God is not *the author* of confusion but of peace, as in all the churches of the saints.

Corinthians 7:9 Now I rejoice, not that you were made sorry, but that your sorrow led to repentance. For you were made sorry in a godly manner, that you might suffer loss from us in nothing.

2 Corinthians 10:4-5 For the weapons of our warfare *are* not carnal but mighty in God for pulling down strongholds, [5] casting down arguments and every high thing that exalts itself against the knowledge of God, bringing every thought into captivity to the obedience of Christ,

Galatians 1:6-8 I marvel that you are turning away so soon from Him who called you in the grace of Christ, to a different gospel, [7] which is not another; but there are some who trouble you and want to pervert the gospel of Christ. [8] But even if we, or an angel from heaven, preach any other gospel to you than what we have preached to you, let him be accursed.

Ephesians 6:12 For we do not wrestle against flesh and blood, but against principalities, against powers, against the rulers of the darkness of this age, against spiritual *hosts* of wickedness in the heavenly *places.*

Philippians 2:9 Therefore God also has highly exalted Him and given Him the name which is above every name,

Philippians 2:12 Therefore, my beloved, as you have always obeyed, not as in my presence only, but now much more in my absence, work out your own salvation with fear and trembling;

Philippians 3:3 For we are the circumcision, who worship God in the Spirit, rejoice in Christ Jesus, and have no confidence in the flesh,

Colossians 1:13 He has delivered us from the power of darkness and conveyed *us* into the kingdom of the Son of His love,

Colossians 2:15 Having disarmed principalities and powers, He made a public spectacle of them, triumphing over them in it.

1 Timothy 4:1 Now the Spirit expressly says that in latter times some will depart from the faith, giving heed to deceiving spirits and doctrines of demons,

2 Timothy 1:7 For God has not given us a spirit of fear, but of power and of love and of a sound mind.

2 Timothy 3:1-7 But know this, that in the last days perilous times will come: [2] For men will be lovers of themselves, lovers of money, boasters, proud, blasphemers, disobedient to parents, unthankful, unholy, [3] unloving, unforgiving, slanderers, without self-control, brutal, despisers of good, [4] traitors, headstrong, haughty, lovers of pleasure rather than lovers of God, [5] having a

form of godliness but denying its power. And from such people turn away! ⁶ For of this sort are those who creep into households and make captives of gullible women loaded down with sins, led away by various lusts, ⁷ always learning and never able to come to the knowledge of the truth.

2 Timothy 4:3 For the time will come when they will not endure sound doctrine, but according to their own desires, *because* they have itching ears, they will heap up for themselves teachers;

2 Timothy 4:18 And the Lord will deliver me from every evil work and preserve *me* for His heavenly kingdom. To Him *be* glory forever and ever. Amen!

Hebrews 4:15-16 For we do not have a High Priest who cannot sympathize with our weaknesses, but was in all *points* tempted as *we are, yet* without sin. ¹⁶ Let us therefore come boldly to the throne of grace, that we may obtain mercy and find grace to help in time of need.

Hebrews 11:25 choosing rather to suffer affliction with the people of God than to enjoy the passing pleasures of sin,

James 3:16 For where envy and self-seeking *exist,* confusion and every evil thing *are* there.

James 5:16 Confess *your* trespasses to one another, and pray for one another, that you may be healed. The effective, fervent prayer of a righteous man avails much.

1 Peter 5:7 casting all your care upon Him, for He cares for you.

Revelation 2:21 And I gave her time to repent of her sexual immorality, and she did not repent.

Revelation 9:6 In those days men will seek death and will not find it; they will desire to die, and death will flee from them.

Revelation 12:11 And they overcame him by the blood of the Lamb and by the word of their testimony, and they did not love their lives to the death.

Revelation 14:7 saying with a loud voice, "Fear God and give glory to Him, for the hour of His judgment has come; and worship Him who made heaven and earth, the sea and springs of water."

Revelation 19:5 Then a voice came from the throne, saying, "Praise our God, all you His servants and those who fear Him, both small and great!"

Revelation 21:8 But the cowardly, unbelieving, abominable, murderers, sexually immoral, sorcerers, idolaters, and all liars shall have their part in the lake which burns with fire and brimstone, which is the second death."

I would like to personally thank you for reading this book. I realize this book was intense but hell is intense, what Christ did for us was intense, and spiritual warfare is intense. I have written 2 other books. My first book is called A PSYCHIC DISCOVERS JESUS. This book goes in to great detail about my life and how I got saved. My second book is called SUICIDE SPIRIT. In this book it goes in to great detail explaining the demonic powers that leads a person to suicide and it explains why the suicide spirit is so hard to rebuke and fight in warfare. I am always open to where the spirit of God wants me to speak at. My web sight is http://exposingthedarkness.com/ If you would like to contact me for a speaking engagement, questions, or just pray please contact me at <u>timthompson74@gmail.com</u> or you can write me a letter at, Tim Thompson p.o. box 701261 Tulsa, Ok 74170 If you would like to help support this ministry it would be greatly appreciated, so you can send it right to the p.o.box also. Once again thank you and have a blessed day, Tim.......